MT4
High Probability
Forex Trading
Method

JIM BROWN

DISCLAIMER

This book is designed to provide information that the author believes to be accurate on the subject matter it covers, but it is sold with the understanding that neither the author nor the publisher is offering individualized advice tailored to any specific portfolio or to any individual's particular needs, or rendering investment advice or other professional services such as legal accounting advice. Professional services should be sought if one needs expert assistance in areas that include investment, legal, and accounting advice. There is a substantial risk of loss associated with trading these markets. Losses can and will occur. No system or methodology has ever been developed that can guarantee profits or ensure freedom from losses. No representation or implication is being made that using this information will generate profits or ensure freedom from losses. The trade examples provided were hypothetical only and were prepared with the benefit of hindsight. No hypothetical trading record can completely account for the impact of financial risk in actual live trading. Additionally, this book is not intended to serve as the basis for any financial decisions, as a recommendation of a specific trading system. Your personal financial circumstances must be considered carefully before investing or spending money. No warranty is made with respect to the accuracy or completeness of the information contained herein, and both the author and the publisher specifically disclaim any responsibility for any liability, loss or risk, personal or otherwise, which is incurred as a consequence, directly or indirectly, of the use and application of any of the contents of this book.

CONTENTS

1

INTRODUCTION

I am a full time Forex Trader. This book will provide you with a reliable and robust trading method which I refined over many months of manual and demo testing, and now live trading. I use the very popular MetaTrader platform to trade. This is more commonly referred to as MT4 and there are many reputable brokers that offer this platform.

Although I concentrate solely on Forex trading myself, I see no reason why you could not trade this method on other financial instruments offered by many MT4 brokers. These may include: oil, precious metals, commodities, stock indices or even individual stocks. There is a great deal on offer and I appreciate that not everyone is a fan of Forex trading.

This particular trading method can be traded on any time frame you choose. Personally, I prefer the 4hr charts or the Daily charts. These are time frames I am comfortable with, but again I understand that there are different strokes for different folks when it comes to time availability, preferred time frames and lifestyle choices etc. I will endeavor to show a few trade examples from different time frames to cover all of the bases.

You will need access to MT4 to use this method as it relies on the use of custom indicators which I had specifically built for this platform. You may not wish to conduct your actual trading off an MT4 platform but you will need to at least download a free demonstration version to enable you to conduct your trade analysis, and you could then place your actual trades on your own preferred broker's platform.

If you do choose to open a live account with a MT4 broker, before making your decision on which broker to go with, I would like to recommend that you contact Justin and his staff at Forest Park FX.

They will be able to match a reputable broker to your specific needs. It does not cost anything as they are compensated by the broker, and to make things even better, there is a chance that you may actually receive cash rebates back into your brokerage account as a result. I am not affiliated at all with Forest Park FX. I am however, a very happy customer and I would not recommend them otherwise.

As you have purchased the paperback version of this book, *I have made the Kindle version on Amazon, available for you to download for free*. If you don't own a Kindle, a free Kindle app can be used for iOS, Windows, Android etc. The electronic version will allow you to tap/double tap on the images and expand them even more if you would like to look at them closer.

2

CUSTOM INDICATORS REQUIRED

As stated previously, there are a number of custom indicators required to trade this method. These custom indicators are as follows and will be provided with the downloadable package at the end of the book:

1. MACD Platinum
2. QQE Adv
3. QMP Filter

If any readers would like to build their own custom indicators based on these MT4 coded indicators, I would be happy to share the source code with you so you could arrange your own Programmer to build something similar on a platform of your choice.

The method also involves the use of multiple Moving Averages. These are a default indicator that can be found on just about any platform. Traders have been using these for years, as they stand the test of time.

I will also supply you with an MT4 template that you can add to your platform which will ensure your charts look the same as mine. It is up to the individual whether you want to use this, or whether you would rather design your own (you may not like my dark charts). In the downloadable package, I have also included a customized Excel spreadsheet to assist you with multiple trades if you are trading a specific way that I will mention later in the book. I have also added one other custom MT4 indicator called the i-ParamonWorkTime which may also be helpful when trading specific times of the day. It is not essential to the method, but it can make things a little easier.

If you are unsure how to load custom indicators or a template on the MT4 platform, you can access my YouTube video at:

https://youtu.be/Ymuxe_X32vM

(case sensitive)

It is very simple if you follow the instructions. That particular video was in relation to a method from my first book, Forex Trading: The Basics Explained in Simple Terms and the principles are basically the same where you have custom indicators and a template to load onto the MT4 platform.

Mac Users

I am not a Mac user myself, but another person informed me that he hit a snag installing the templates after watching the YouTube clip. He found that he couldn't drag the Modified MACD template across.

In the end, he used a program called PlayonMac to get the MT4 platform, but when he couldn't get it to recognize the file he discovered he had to copy and paste it from the folder in the wine library to the folder that's also in the wine library. You can't transfer it straight from your file.

I am sorry I can't elaborate on this further - these are his words and I hope it helps. If not, I can ask whether there is a Mac user in my Facebook group who can help some more.

3

MY THOUGHTS ABOUT INDICATORS

Many will tell you that all indicators lag. What they mean by this is that they react or present after price has already moved so they are too late to the party because price has moved, leaving the indicators behind. There is probably some truth in this, especially if you were looking at a Moving Average cross or something similar. But please do not discount the use of indicators. When used in conjunction with each other they can prove very beneficial. Also keep in mind that the same people that criticize indicators as lagging, more than likely rely on price action for their trading signals. And as you have probably heard me say before, price is king, but that is not to say price won't blow through any support and resistance level, fib level, trend line or Elliot Wave analysis that the price action trader is relying on. Both methods have their advantages and disadvantages.

No one, and I repeat, no one knows where price is going next!

What we are trying to do however, is give ourselves an edge. We all try and trade a method that we are comfortable with, practice it thoroughly and become so in tune with it that it becomes second nature to us. Well, that is the plan anyway. What works exceptionally well for one trader may be a complete dog to another trader - this is just the way it is. We are all made up of different opinions, thought processes, risk tolerance, mental capacity and other factors that mold you as a trader.

What I am offering is a simple mechanical trading method. I prefer definite rules for entry and I like to see some sort of indicator, or sequence of events, on a chart that tells me when to enter ie. No second guessing the entry. I am not too concerned about exits, as there are many factors to help determine that process, which I will cover in more detail later in the book with trade examples. However, I do want to see my entry in black and white as that makes it easier for me, as I am sure it does for a lot of other traders as well. A favorite saying of mine when it comes to trading is *Patience,*

Courage and Discipline'. You must patiently wait for the correct trade set up and when it presents, you have to have the courage to take it. The discipline refers to the whole package, where you follow your method to the letter and also ensure that other factors that affect your trading are adhered to. This may include money management, general health and wellbeing, sleep, meditation, affirmations etc. Namely, the whole package!

4

TRADING WITH THE TREND AND TREND IDENTIFICATION

Some of the most successful trading methods trade pullbacks or retracements in a major trend, and that is exactly what this does. So, if the market is an up trend we wait for small pullbacks (or retracements) to the down side and then look for an entry to buy again, as we are counting on the up trend continuing. It is the exact opposite for a down trend, where we wait for pullbacks (or retracements) back to the up side and then look for an entry to sell again, as we are counting on the down trend continuing. But having said that, you could also trade this against the major trend if you so desired. Although, why swim against the tide?

So how do we identify a major trend? The easiest way is to use a combination of indicators and I will provide you with my set up. Basically I determine a trend on the chart by using 3x Moving Averages. I use the 50 EMA, 100 EMA and 240 LMA. EMA stands for Exponential Moving Average and LMA stands for Linear Weighted Moving Average. You can use whatever you like to determine a trend, whether that be MAs or one of your own favorite methods. It is up to you, but I prefer the MAs myself.

I look for the MAs to be stacked so that there is an obvious trend either up or down. If you refer to the screenshots for examples, you will notice that it is very easy to see the trend when you put them on the charts. You will be surprised how often the MAs are stacked so there are plenty of trading opportunities. If they aren't, then simply ignore that pair and check out other pairs.

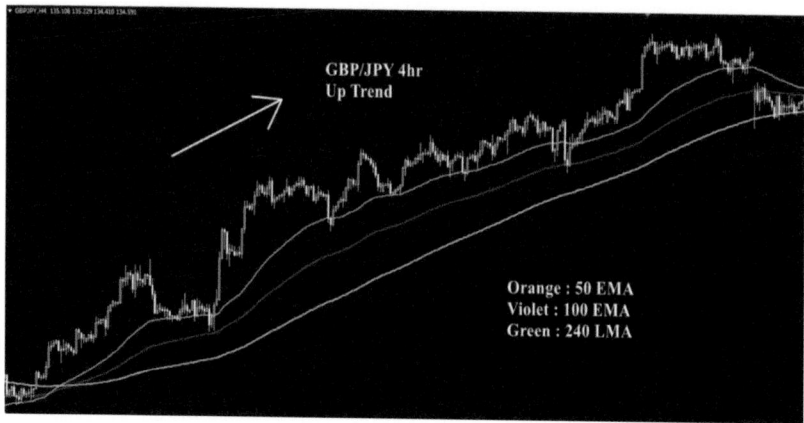

Figure 1. MAs Stacked in an Up Trend

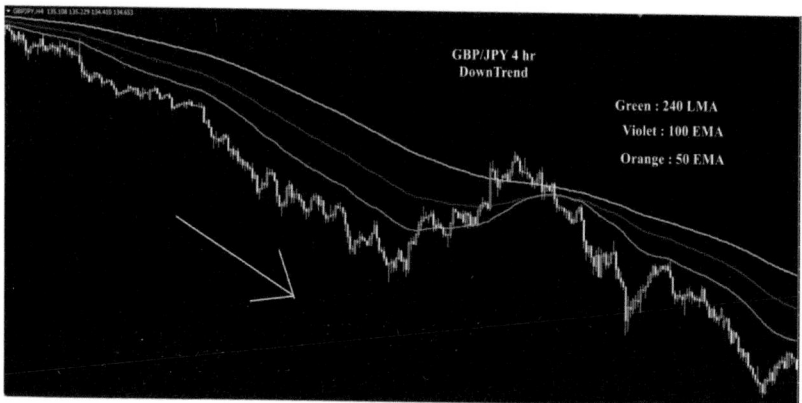

Figure 2. MAs Stacked in a Down Trend

You could use the MAs to determine the trend and that would be fine, but I like to add a further confirmation. This is especially the case if I am trading the 1hr charts or smaller time frames like the 5m, 15m or 30m charts where I use the QMP Filter, which has a higher time frame filter built into it. First however, I will explain how the QMP Filter works. It is a custom indicator that is actually displayed on the price chart itself that I designed to make my life a little easier from a visual point of view.

What I mean by this is that the QMP Filter is made up of a combination of the MACD Platinum and the QQE Adv custom indicators. All of my trade signals are based on a cross of the QQE Adv with default settings of 1,8,3 and the red or blue dots on the MACD Platinum with default settings of

12,26,9. The crossing on the QQE Adv has to be in sync with the relevant colored dot on the MACD Platinum. The easiest way to see this is to put all three custom indicators on the chart and use the platform's crosshair to identify the signals. Sometimes the cross on the QQE Adv is at the same time a red or blue form on the MACD Platinum but not always, so instead of trying to line them up all of the time, I had the QMP Filter built to identify where exactly they were in sync by the use of the colored dots.

For this trading method to work, you don't actually need to display the QQE Adv on your charts, but you have to have it loaded onto your platform to ensure the QMP Filter works. You will need to display the MACD Platinum though, as it is a part of the actual trade analysis used by this method. If you choose to use my template, then everything will be displayed correctly. But if you choose not to use the template, when you load the MACD Platinum onto the charts you will have to go into the settings and change a couple of things:

- Go to the 'inputs' tab and change 'ShowMarkers' to true so you will see the dots on the indicator.

- Change 'MarkerColorUp' to Dodger Blue so you have the same color as me.

- Go into the 'colors' tab of the QMP Filter and change #0 to Dodger Blue, and #2 and #3 to Yellow.

5

WHAT YOUR CHART SHOULD LOOK LIKE

If you have used my template then your chart should look like the next screenshot. That is, if you have used a 4hr chart or smaller. If you have it on a Daily chart or higher, then you will not see the yellow arrows as the template is set up to use a Daily chart as a filter.

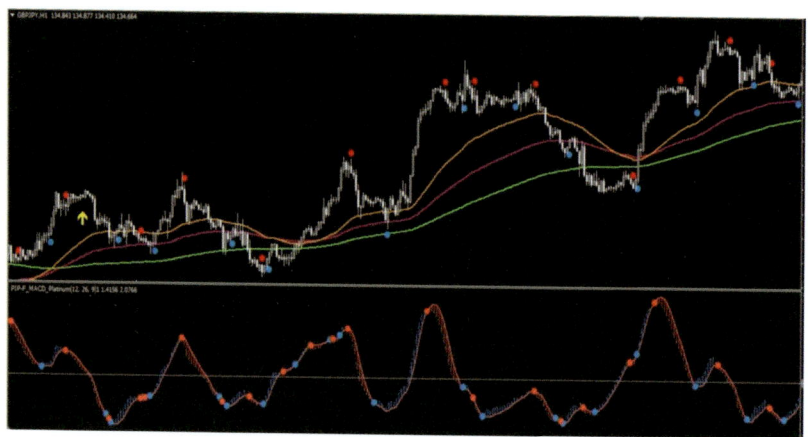

Figure 3. Example of my Template on a 1hr Chart

This shows a 1hr chart with the full set up. The yellow arrows refer to a Daily chart set up if I was using the QMP Filter on that time frame. So basically, an upward pointing yellow arrow would represent a blue dot on the Daily chart if I had added the QMP Filter to it, and a downward pointing yellow arrow would represent a red dot on the Daily chart. I used an arrow to stand out from the current time frame's red and blue dots.

To set the higher time frame filter on the QMP Filter so you can see the yellow arrows, go into the 'inputs tab' of the indicator and in the field called

'HigherTimeFrame', input your desired setting which is always displayed in minutes. If you don't want to use it, leave it blank or put in the time frame of the chart you are using or a smaller number. But if you were on the 1hr chart and want to use the 4hr chart as a filter, then you would have to put 240 in this field, as there are 240 minutes in 4hrs. Other settings would be 1440 for a day, 10080 for a week and 43200 for a month. As mentioned, this is always in minutes.

In a nutshell, if the Moving Averages were stacked to the upside and there was an upward pointing yellow arrow, then I have two trend confirming scenarios, therefore I would only prefer to take buy trades on the 1hr chart. If the Moving Averages were stacked down and there was a downward pointing yellow arrow, then I would look at sell trades only on the 1hr chart. Trading with the trend. But all trends come to an end eventually and I will discuss this later. If you had conflicting signals, then you may choose to step aside and look at another pair or wait for a clearer trend.

6

LOOKING FOR TRADE ENTRIES

Once we have established the trend, it is time to look for some trade entries. If the chart was in an up (buy) trend, then we are looking for blue dots forming on the MACD Platinum below the zero level. This is a heads up advising that there is a possible buy trade very soon. We will only take the trade once a QMP Filter blue dot is confirmed.

Generally the MACD Platinum dots will display before a QMP Filter blue dot, but every now and then, they will be at the same time. Once the QMP Filter blue dot is confirmed by the closing of the current candle, the buy trade would be taken on the open of the new candle. The actual QMP Filter dots will not appear mid candle, so you won't see them until a candle actually closes. If you did want a warning of an impending dot, then you could simply add the QQE Adv indicator to your chart which would provide you with a very good idea on when a QMP Filter dot will appear as you will clearly see an impending cross on this indicator, keeping in mind that the QMP Filter is a combination of the MACD Platinum dots and the cross of the QQE Adv that then displays the red or blue dot on the price chart.

In a down (sell) trend on the chart, we would be looking for red dots forming on the MACD Platinum above the zero level, and then looking for a confirmed red dot on the QMP Filter. Same as a buy trade but in reverse.

I have supplied you with all the indicators and also a template and I strongly suggest that you place the template on a few charts with different time frames and have a look at the potential set ups. It works the majority of the time and it will give you a good framework to possibly build your own trading system around.

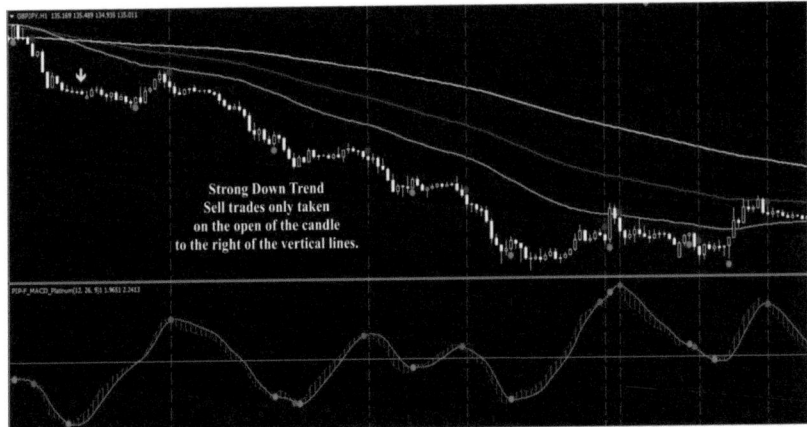

Figure 4. Example showing sell trades

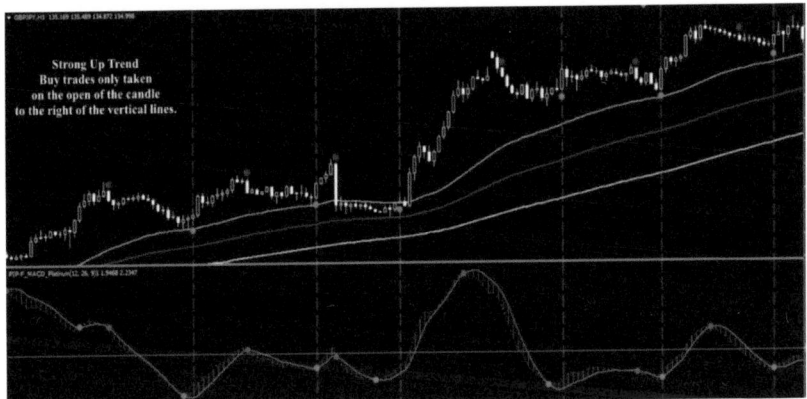

Figure 5. Example showing buy trades

You will be impressed how simple the method is and the large number of successful trades that it produces, but like any trading system, it is not perfect. So I will now discuss a few ideas on trade management and some of the pitfalls of trading this way.

There are a few different options on how you could trade this method and I will discuss a low risk method that is based on a more traditional way of trading, and also a slightly different method that has a higher risk and adds to your position size if things go against you.

7

METHOD NO. 1 (LOWER RISK)

The low risk way to trade this method is to take the buy and sell signals with the trend and then place a stop on each trade at a relevant point according to your own analysis based on your money management strategy. For example, you may wish to place a hard stop just above/below the high/low of the signal candle, or at a recent fractal, or the other side of one of the MAs. The choice is yours. You could then manage the open trade by various means, whether that is via a hard profit target, trailing stop, or some other level like Fibs, Support and Resistance, Pivot Levels etc. Again the choice is yours, but I will cover some ideas that will let you know when the trend is exhausted.

Every buy or sell signal is treated as an individual trade where they are managed separately. Stops will generally be fairly tight so you will know what your risk is at all times. In a perfect scenario, you would see one dot on MACD Platinum either side of the zero level where it basically goes from sell to buy to sell to buy to sell etc. This makes for easy trading, especially if you are trading in one direction only.

When the trend does eventually change direction, your stop will get you out completely and there will be no new trades taken until a new trend is identified, or the original trend resumes. Or you could trade from each side of the MACD Platinum if the trend is flat or undecided. Whichever way you choose to identify your trades, this is the smart way to trade this method and certainly the safest.

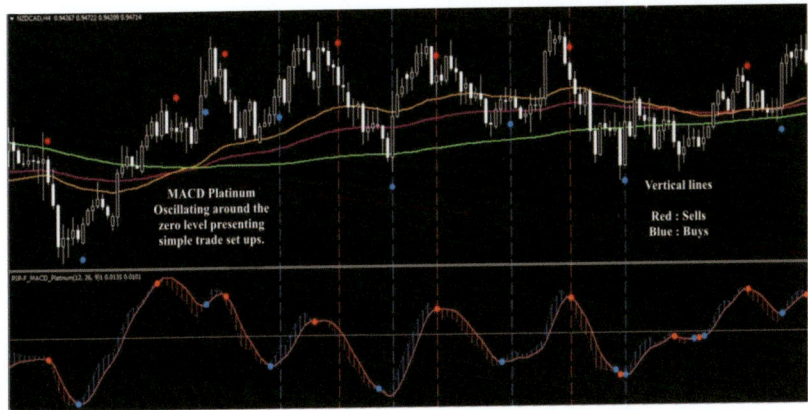

Figure 6. Example of going from trade to trade on MACD Platinum

8

METHOD NO. 2 (HIGHER RISK)

First, I must warn you that this method requires excellent money management skills as you will be adding to a possible losing position. It is not for everyone but it can work quite well if you are disciplined and smart about your money management. So here, instead of setting a hard stop loss on my initial trade, I will either enter with no stop loss at all, or at least have a major catastrophe stop loss set quite a distance from entry. The thing is you never know when a trend is going to end so there may be times when you are caught on the wrong side of it. If using Method No. 1 mentioned above, then it really will not be a problem, but using this alternate Method No. 2 may cause you some grief.

Here is how it works. I will use an example of a sell trade. You are with the trend and your see a red dot on the MACD Platinum that is above the zero level and is confirmed by a red dot on the QMP Filter, so you take the sell trade with 1x unit (eg 0.1 lot). But instead of price heading down, it heads up, where you then see a blue dot on the MACD Platinum above the zero level, and this is confirmed by a blue dot on the QMP Filter. Your sell trade is not looking too healthy now!

But then price turns down again, where there is another red dot on the MACD Platinum which is still above the zero level, and this is then confirmed by another red dot on the QMP Filter. Here you take another sell trade, but this time it is for 3x units (eg 0.3 lots). There is still no hard stop in place, but you may wish to place a catastrophe stop some distance away, just in case. Now you are short 4x units (eg 0.4 lots) in total on this one sequence of trades. Now if price heads up again and you went through the same scenario with blue dots followed by red dots whilst still in the selling area, then a third sell would be opened for 5x units (eg 0.5 lots).

Now you can see why money management is important as you have to be able to add to your position exponentially. It is like a Fib sequence of 1,3,5,8,13,21,34 etc. You do not really want to get that high but, it could happen.

Figure 7. Example of multiple sell trades

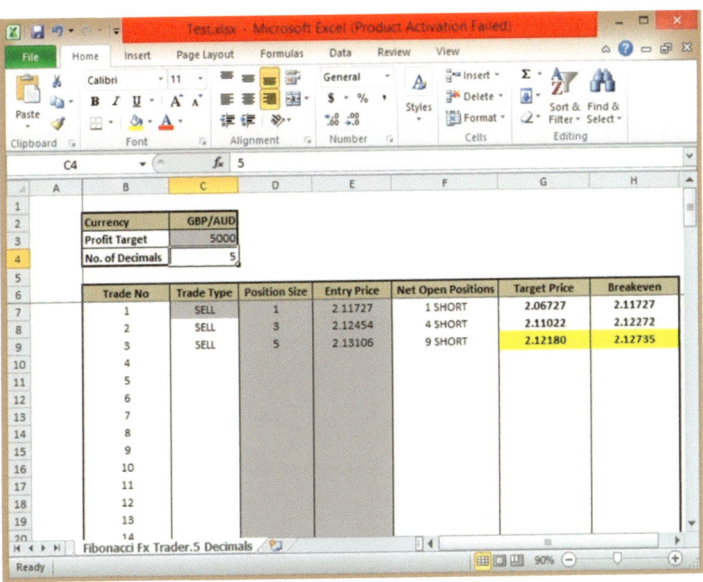

Figure 8. Inputs for the trades in Figure 7

If you then had three sell trades on the same pair at 0.1, 0.3 and 0.5 lots, you would be net short 0.9 lots. Here, you want to treat all of these trades as a part of a sequence or a basket of trades. The downloadable content will provide you with a basic custom made Excel spreadsheet where you can enter the details of all your trades and this in turn will calculate an overall break-even point or even an overall target of your choice based on the initial entry, which in this example was 0.1 lot. The spreadsheet does the math for you as long (as you enter the data correctly).

Figure 9. Example of multiple Buy trades

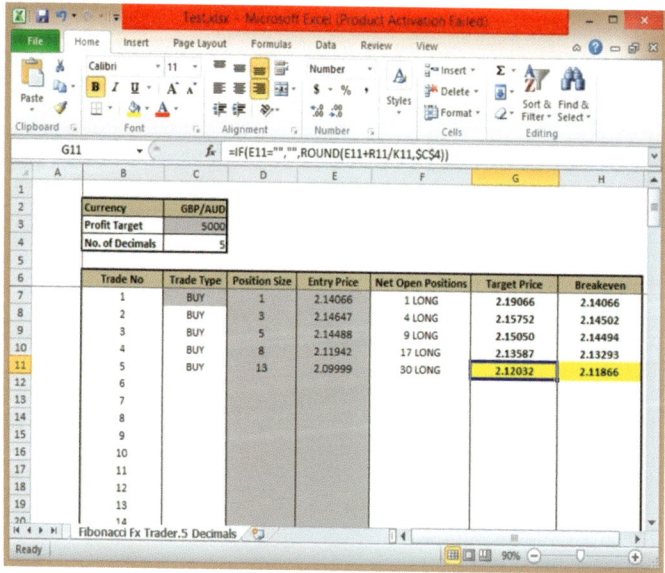

Figure 10. Inputs for trades in Figure 9

In Figure 9, I would not be too comfortable with so many trades open in one direction and I would be continuously looking for ways to reduce my overall risk. For example, there was an opportunity to get out at overall break even after trade no.4 was taken – and this is what I would be looking for.

If you missed the opportunity to exit, then trade no.5 would need to be taken, and it would be a confident trade to take due to the large bullish divergence created between trades 4 and 5. Price is heading much lower however the MACD Platinum is heading higher, therefore it is highly likely that price will turn up also. Which in hindsight, we can clearly see that it did.

Even if you managed to exit after trade no.4 at overall break even, trade no.5 would have been an excellent stand-alone trade anyway. And notice how small a distance price had to travel from the break-even level to achieve +500 pips if all five trades were open? This is due to the large overall position size on at the time. However, would you be able to handle the stress, keeping in mind that the MACD Platinum was still below the zero level and therefore still a valid buy trade scenario?

9

THE THEORY BEHIND THE METHOD

The theory behind the whole method is that the MACD Platinum tends to want to come back to the zero level when it extends away from it on either side. Think of it as a rubber band whereby the more you stretch it out, the more pressure there is for it to come back to its natural state. Look at most charts and you will see the MACD Platinum continuously going from one side of the zero level to the other and then back. Is it a reversion to the mean? Is it an overbought/oversold oscillator? I am not sure, but it is fairly consistent on how it performs.

If you looked at pairs like the NZD/CAD, which is a low volatility pair most of the time, you could probably take every trade in every direction without having to worry about trend direction too much. This is especially true on the higher time frames. But then you look at a pair like GBP/JPY that can make huge moves in one direction, and even though it is going from one side of the zero level to the other side on the MACD Platinum, this pair could be in a huge move heading in one direction only, so obviously it is best to go with the trend here.

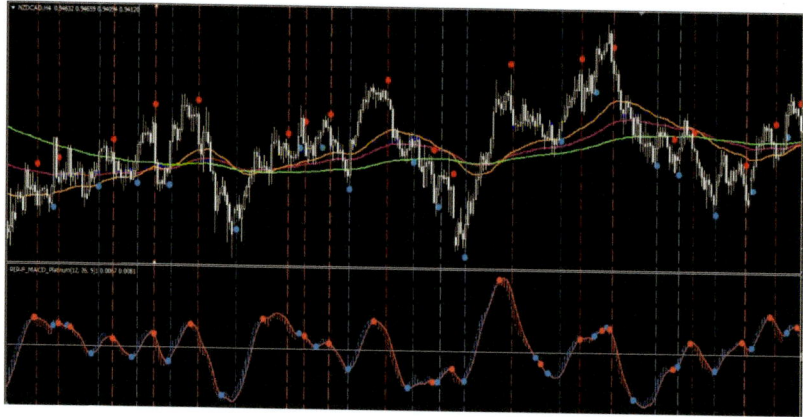

Figure 11. Multiple trades on the NZD/CAD

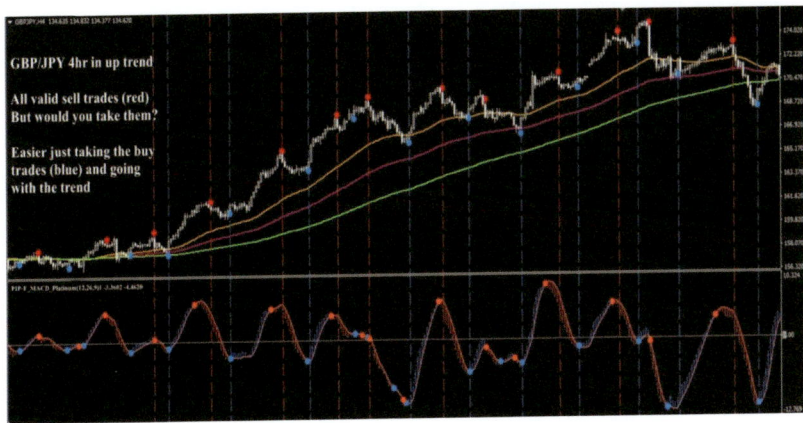

Figure 12. Multiple trades on the GBP/JPY

One thing I want to make clear here is that I am providing you with a framework of a trading method. This is something you can take and make your own. You may not be comfortable trading the same way as I do or you may not agree with how I determine trend. I am totally comfortable with that as I encourage you to find your own way to trade. You can take my ideas, or use my indicators and even add your own ideas. I am fine with that, and that is how I want you to think. But having said that, if you ran with what I present here in this book, then that is also fine.

Whichever path you take in trading, my advice to you is to be comfortable with at least one trading method and become really good at it. You have to live and breathe it, where you are ready for anything as you recognize the patterns or the moves your particular financial instrument makes. The best way to achieve this is a combination of historical chart time and also by forward testing, whether that be on a demo account or a small live account. Do not even consider risking serious money until you are proficient and comfortable with the method you are using.

10

THINGS TO CONSIDER USING METHOD NO. 1 (LOWER RISK)

Here are some things to consider if you were using the Method No.1 type of way to trade. It appears that the trading signals are stronger when price has actually come into the MAs or has recently touched the MAs. Therefore, if price is a long way from the closest MA and there is a new trade signal, then it may pay not to take that trade as generally price will want to come back to the MAs so there may be a better entry at a future time. You do not have to take every trade, just the ones that look like a good set up to you.

Figure 13. Example of price coming back into MAs in an up trend

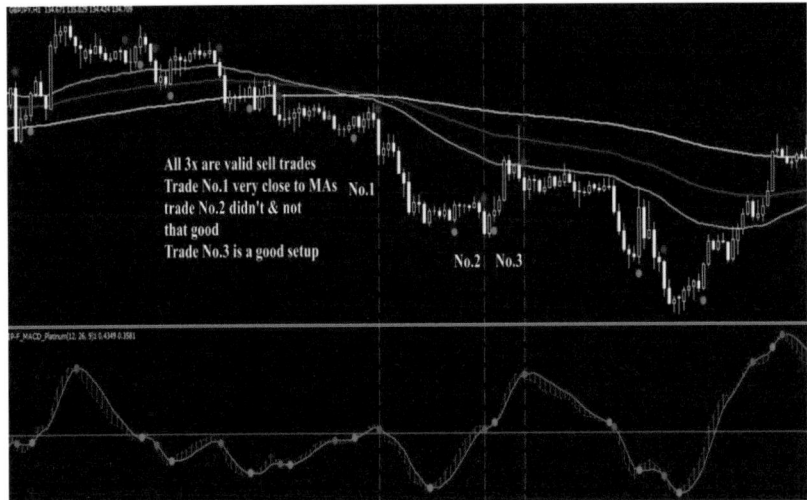

Figure 14. Another example of price coming back into MAs in a down trend

Another option may be to draw trend lines on the charts and only take the identified signals when a trend line is broken. Now whether this is a trend line from the chart time frame you are trading, or even a higher time frame, it is up to you. Trend lines can be a great tool if used correctly. With drawing trend lines, don't get caught up with being too precise.

There are different schools of thought out there on how they should be drawn. Pick one way and stick with it. As I use candles on all of my charts, I generally go from an extreme high or low and then use the top or bottom of the main candle body for my touching points, ignoring the wicks (or shadows as they are sometimes called). This works for me, but would probably have some perfectionists pulling their hair out.

Do what is easy for you. Figure 15 and Figure 16 on the following page, both show the use of a trend line break to enter a counter trend trade.

Figure 15. Trend line break for a Sell trade

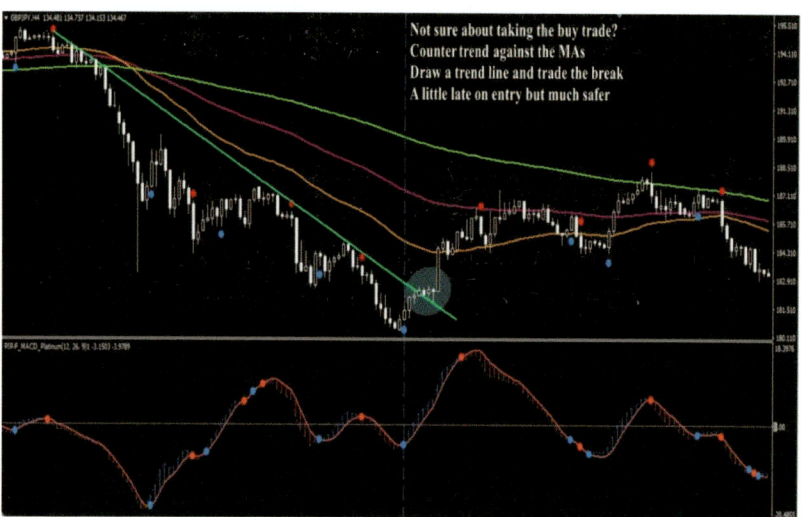

Figure 16. Trend line break for a Buy trade

11

DIVERGENCE

And now onto something you will often see when trading this chart set up: Divergence.

This can be a very powerful confirmation tool. Divergence means a difference between actual price and the MACD Platinum indicator, where they appear to be heading in different directions. The following screenshots provide examples of what divergence actually looks like and how to help you use it in your trading. Even though it can be quite reliable as a stand-alone signal, I would be reluctant to use it without any other type of confirmation. But it is something very powerful and something I am always watching for. I look for standard divergence, as described above. There is something called hidden divergence but it is a little trickier to spot and I do not personally look for it. But, it may be something you would like to add to your trading arsenal.

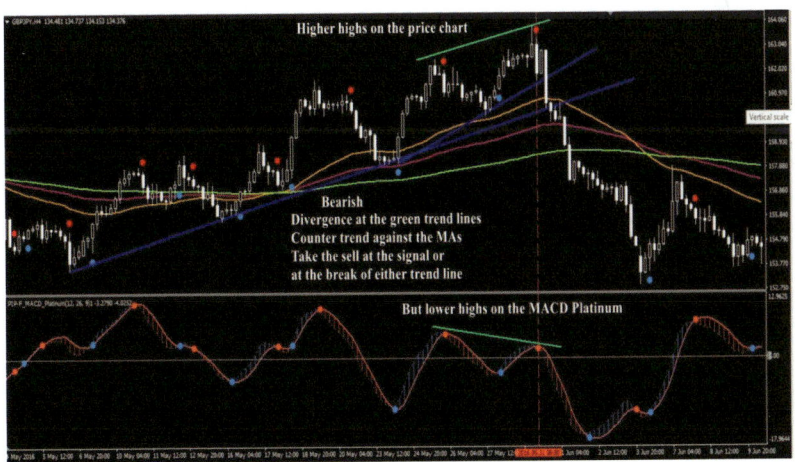

Figure 17. Example of bearish divergence

Figure 18. Example of bullish divergence

I appreciate that there are traders who rely on other methods for entry. These may include candlestick patterns, Elliot Wave analysis, Gann analysis, support and resistance levels, Fib levels, Pivot levels, or even different phases of the moon. Whatever your thing is, feel free to use that, but have a look at what I am offering here and you may be able to incorporate it into your own method and they may actually complement each other. I personally like to throw my Fib tool on the Daily charts as it provides a good idea of where price is at or where it may head next. The very first trading method I learnt was on basic Gann analysis where it was based on swings and retracements, so it is something I still look at these days.

12

TRADE MANAGEMENT AND EXIT

Contrary to popular belief, the entry is really not that critical. Sure you would like to think you have selected the correct trade direction right from the get go, and that is generally your plan. But it is really not that important. Trade management and exit are very important however. This is where the good traders are distinguished from the not so good traders. We have all heard that we should cut our losers quickly and let our winners run. Well this is actually quite true and should be adhered to if you are trading in a more traditional style. And as we all know, this is much easier said than done! Human nature does not like us to lose, so you tend to hang on to the losers, but it also wants us to take a winner when it presents, so we tend to close those winning trades out early.

There are a couple of different schools of thought with regards to risk to reward ratios, scaling in, scaling out, hard profit targets, trailing stops etc. Do not listen to the crowd or be influenced by others. Do your own testing and do what is right for you. Trading involves mind games, or the psychological side of things, and it will mess with you at times. You will make decisions under pressure and then look back on them later and question why you made that decision. Well, get used to it as happens to the best of us. It is amazing the stupid things you will do when there is a relevant amount of money on the line. Do what works best for you so you can keep your heart rate at a reasonable level. We all make mistakes, and the trick is to learn from them so you don't make the same mistake again. Okay, maybe once more, but if you make it a third time, it is time to re-assess.

Where to place your stops? That is up to you. I've already given you a few ideas earlier in the book when I was touched on the more traditional style of trading when using this method (Method No.1), where you pick and choose your trades and they are all treated as individual trades. I suggested areas like a recent fractal, which is a recent high or low. Or even a certain distance above/below the signal candle, which is the candle the QMP Filter signal dot appeared on. You may wish to use a more technical recent high or low that may be further away from the entry area. The Moving Averages may be in a suitable area for stop placement, as could be Fib levels, Pivot levels, a trend line or any other indicator/object of your choice. The choices are endless, but remember your money management rules with regards to placement.

Figure 19. Examples of simple stop placement

I will not go into depth regarding money management as it is a major subject in itself and this book would not do it justice. However I will cover some basics. You will hear a great deal about how much you should risk on any one trade and the most common seems to be around 1% to 2% of your account balance. You can't really go wrong if you follow that one simple rule.

To make things easier, you could use a simple and freely available position size calculator like this one at http://www.myfxbook.com/forex-calculators/position-size which makes the math very easy. But be aware when you have multiple trades on the same pair, as you would have to look at overall risk on that basket of trades. This would be the case when trading Method No.2.

Also if you are trading highly correlated pairs, you may be increasing your risk without realizing. There is plenty of excellent information available regarding money management and how to incorporate it into your trading plan, so I would strongly suggest that you take time to do some research and make sensible decisions based on that. The trick in trading is if you have one or more losses, you will have enough capital to continue trading another day. In other words, keep your position size small and manageable. If you can't sleep at night with open trades going against you, then you are probably trading way too big.

13

RE-ENTRIES AND USE OF TREND LINES

Now back to the trading. There may be times when you are stopped out and the original buy or sell signal remains intact. It could have been that your original stop was too tight or it could have been the old, taken out by 1x pip scenario where the broker is out to get us (highly unlikely, but that is how some traders think). But if this is the case, don't write off that trading opportunity as you may be in a position to look for a re-entry.

This could be achieved by placing a Buy or Sell Stop order, so if price does go back in your favor, you are automatically taken back into the same trade set up. Or you may wish to use a trend line here and wait for a confirmed break of that trend line for a re-entry, again in the same trade. You may have to re-assess your stop loss position which may in turn require a position size adjustment to fit in with your money management plan.

And a reminder of what the difference is between the different types of orders on the MT4 platform. If you enter a trade immediately at the current price, then that is referred to a Market Order.

Now to the tricky ones, that can be a little confusing. These are the Stop Order or the Limit Order.

> ▪ A Buy Stop Order is where price is currently below your preferred entry point, so you are looking for price to head up and fill your order and then hopefully continue up - sort of picking up the order as momentum picks up.

> ▪ A Buy Limit Order is where price is currently at a certain level, but you want to have your buy order filled below that level. So you are looking for price to first drop down to your entry point, and then once that is filled, you are expecting price to reverse and head up.

• A Sell Stop Order is the exact opposite. Price is already above your order level and you are waiting for it to fall to fill your order on the way through.

• A Sell Limit Order is where price is at a certain level and you want to set an order to sell at a price higher than the current level, looking for a fill followed by a reversal of price to the downside.

A limit order is used at support and resistance levels etc. I rarely use them as I don't know where a market is going to turn, hence I like to pick orders up in the trend direction which is by the use of Stop Orders.

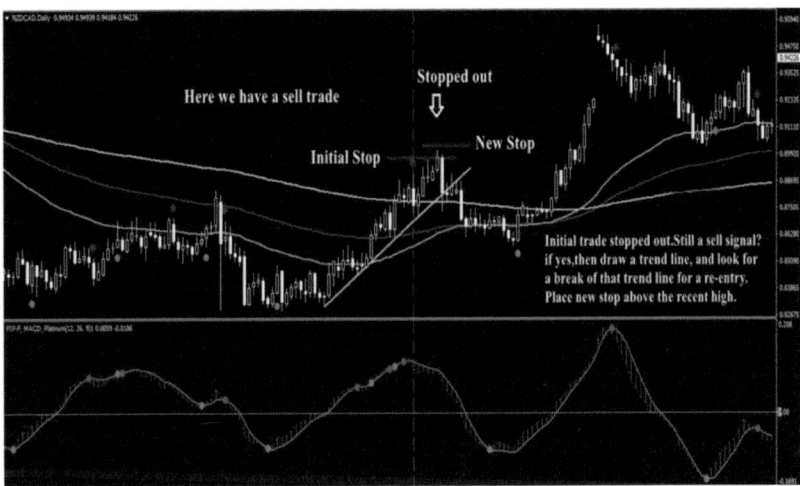

Figure 20. Example of re-entry using a trend line break in a sell trade

Figure 21. Example of re-entry using a trend line break in a buy trade

14

WHEN TO EXIT A TRADE

So, when is a good time to get out of a trade using this method? Again, there are many options. I will mainly cover the more traditional way of trading this method (Method No.1) but some of these ideas will also apply to the higher risk style of trading this (Method No.2), where we are adding to positions. Firstly, let me be quite clear here, no one knows how long a trend will last. I have probably already stated that earlier, but it does need repeating. As far as I am concerned anyone who tells you that they do is simply making an educated guess based on their analysis. Certainly, some traders are very good at this but most are not, so we need to be able to adapt and trade what is presented to us at the time. Be ready for anything.

There are traders that have a set $ target amount for the day/week/month, and once that is achieved they are happy and shut down their charts. Most of us are greedy though and will try and milk as much out of the market as possible. Fair enough I say, as we are all trading to make money so we can enjoy a certain or improved lifestyle. Even though I enjoy trading, I don't live to trade. I enjoy the money and the lifestyle it provides. Traders are capitalists in my opinion as they enjoy the money. Now I would like to think that once you have provided for your family, then you would do something useful for society with regards to the remaining profits. But of course, that is up to the individual.

So, where to take profit or close out? Again, this is your call. How many pips is enough for you? Have you got that specific $ target whereby once that is achieved, you close out all open trades and call it quits? Now I'll give you some tips on how to exit or at least look for specific set ups that may give you a heads up that it is time to consider exiting or at least tightening up your stop.

Most of these are based on the MACD Platinum and how it displays. Remember what I said earlier about it going from one side of the zero level to the other and then back again? This is what I am looking for.

■ If the MACD Platinum crosses the zero level, then this may be your first warning of a possible trend change or if you have enough pips, then simply exit the trade.

■ The MACD Platinum crosses the zero level and then there is an opposite colored dot. Again, either exit the trade or tighten up your stop. If you want to remain in the trade, it may pay to move your stop loss to break even, wait one or two candles, and then move your stop to a better position. Sometimes when a new colored dot appears just on the other side of the zero level of the MACD Platinum, it does not necessarily mean that the original trend has finished, but possibly only a small retracement or pullback.

■ Or when the MACD Platinum crosses the zero level, where you would stay in and only close when the MACD Platinum then crosses the zero level a 2nd time. There are times when you get into a decent trend in your favor where you have locked in some decent profit, and now you want to give the market room to move. This is where you could employ this method.

Figure 22. Examples of exit or stop adjustment based on MACD Platinum position

Figure 23. More examples of exit or stop adjustment based on MACDPlatinum position

Then, you have the more obvious or more traditional ways of exiting.

■ A Trailing Stop. This could either be a certain distance of pips below/above current price, recent highs/lows, a technical level eg Fib level, Pivot level, major support/resistance. Or you may choose something like a 3x candle trail stop strategy. The choices are many and it is your call.

■ A nominated profit target. You may be happy with +50 pips profit on a trade where you close out when that target is achieved. But you may also be targeting a specific level based on some other analysis. One of my favorites can be the 240 LMA at times, if trading against the trend.

This MA can be a real magnet to price. Again you could use the Fib levels, Pivot levels, support/resistance levels. There are many options and the decision is yours. You may be a trader that does work off a certain risk/reward ratio whereas if you risked -50 pips for your stop loss, you may be looking for a +100 pip profit target to justify a 1:2 risk/reward ratio.

■ I am not one for scaling into trades as I am not good at it and I cannot really see the point of it, especially using Method No.1. I guess Method No.2 could be considered scaling in but I like to consider it as more of a rolling up or rolling down scenario. One thing I do like is scaling out of a trade, whether this is in halves or even multiple partial chunks of the original position size.

Generally I will hit an area where I think the market is stalling or the market has moved sufficiently enough for me to justify moving my Stop Loss to break even, where I will close out half or a portion of my position and then move my stop to either the original point of entry or to an overall break even position. Some traders disagree with this method due to the way it can affect your overall risk/reward ratio, but to me I like experiencing some profit locked in and be in an overall 'can't lose' position.

What I am looking for here is for the market to take off where I can cash in on a huge move on the remainder of my position. But probably 7 times out 10, the market will pull back and more than likely take out your remaining position for a smaller profit than the first close, or at break even. I am comfortable doing this as it does wonders for my trading psyche but it may not suit others.

▪ Finally, you can choose to use whatever method that suits you. This could be an indicator, whether a standard or custom indicator, eg Parabolic SAR, ATR levels, standard MACD signal. Or you could exit on a certain scenario being played out, eg MAs cross, price crosses and closes on the other side of an MA, it is the end of the day/week and you want to be flat (nil open trades), major news is being released soon. There are plenty of options.

15

SHORTER TIME FRAME TRADING

I also have some other thoughts to share. If you prefer the shorter time frames like the 5 minute or 15 minute charts, then you may wish to consider only trading at certain times of the day. An example of this may be that you only trade the London or US session only. I prefer the longer time frame trading but I understand the desire for many traders to look at the shorter time frames for various reasons. It may be that you are time poor and can only trade for a limited number of hours every now and then. But if you do have the time and you can monitor the higher time frame charts, then I would strongly suggest you go with them. It may not be as a 'sexy' as being a Day Trader, but trust me, it will be easier and you may be surprised how profitable it can be with less hands on work.

If you must trade the lower time frames, then ensure you are aware of any major news releases coming out during your trading session, especially if it can greatly affect the pair you are trading. I cannot stress this enough. There is no need to get out of open trades, but you have to be ready for anything and then act quickly if things go against you.

A resource that is quite good for the news that can be filtered to suit your time zone and specific requirements is the Forex Factory Calendar, which can be found at http://www.forexfactory.com/calendar.php. Also the MT4 custom indicator called the i-ParamonWorkTime which is a part of your download package is a very useful tool for helping keep track of your trading times. This is a custom indicator that you place on your chart and set it to suit your actual broker's platform time to match your trading session, whereby it will create a different color background on the chart during these times to give you a more visual experience.

Figure 24. Snapshot of the Forex Factory calendar

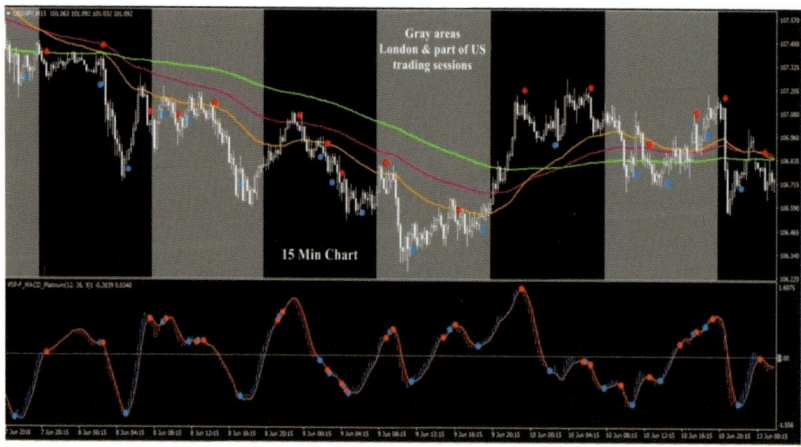

Figure 25. Trading session times on a 15 minute chart using the i-ParamonWorkTime custom indicator

16

COUNTER TREND TRADING

Generally the further the MACD Platinum dot is away from the zero level, the better chance you have of your trade succeeding. This is not always the case, but I like to look for counter trend set ups on the 4hr or Daily charts when this occurs. With these trades, I would suggest you keep it tight and monitor them a bit closer, keeping in mind that you are normally going against the major trend. But having said that, you will experience some very profitable trades as long as you are not being too greedy and expecting too much from them. This is a good way to trade when the MAs are flat or very tight and there is no obvious trend where you can trade from one side of the MACD Platinum to the other and so on, until a new obvious trend is identified.

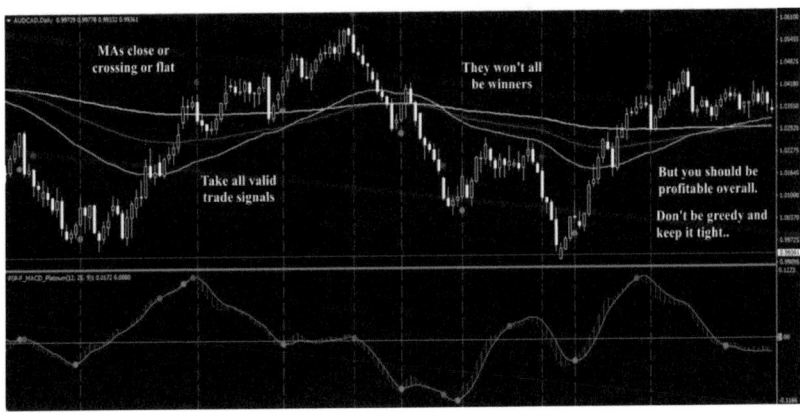

Figure 26. MAs flat and taking all trades in both directions

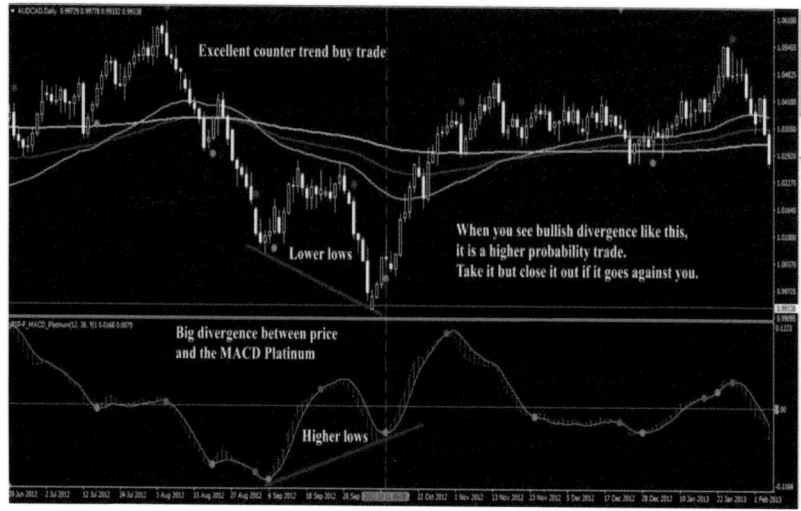

Figure 27. Example of a counter trend trade (divergence)

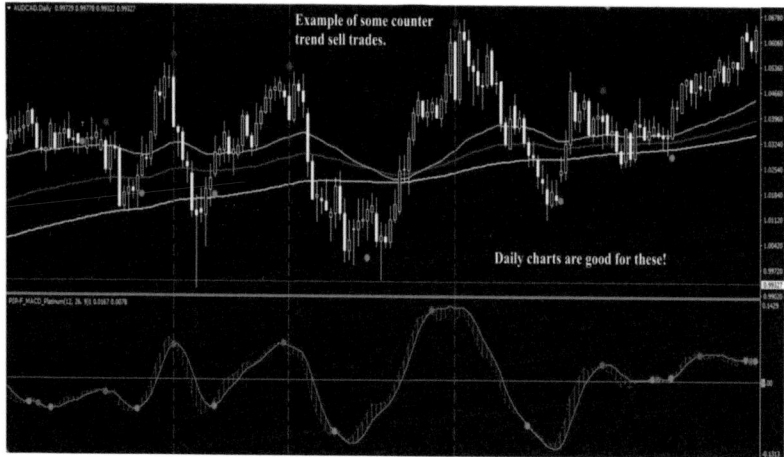

Figure 28. Example of multiple counter trend trades where taking
sells in an up trend

17

TRADE POSITION SIZE

Go in small initially to get a feel for it. Do not be embarrassed trading small lot sizes as you can actually make some decent profit when you get on a roll. You can always increase sizes later when you are comfortable. Use the power of compounding to build an account where you can maintain a constant risk percentage on each trade, and as your account balance grows, your position size will increase without any added risk.

With regards to the Method No.2 where you are taking multiple trades in the same direction and increasing your trade size as the trade rolls out, then you want to start small anyway. I cannot stress enough that money management is critical when trading this way. You have to consider your maximum risk if you have multiple trades on, and there may be a time where an overall break even scenario presents, where closing out all of your trades is the smart thing to do. You can make some huge profits with multiple trades in the same direction when price goes in your favor, but be warned that if price goes against you, then this will also amplify your losses. It is the old double edged sword theory where higher reward normally goes hand in hand with higher risk.

Method No.1 where you treat each entry signal as an individual trade with a stop loss in place is the smart way to trade this system. I was reluctant to mention Method No.2 due to the fact that this would probably be the domain of the more experienced traders due to the issue of possible amplified losses and things getting out of hand if you do not take clear decisive action when certain scenarios present.

For example, there may be a time when you are in 4x buy trades at the same time and things are starting to look a little ugly on the chart, where price momentarily moves to an overall break even position. A smart trader would seize this opportunity to exit all trades and then patiently wait for the next trade set up, whereas a not so smart trader may act like a deer in the headlights and freeze, taking no action, only to watch price reverse keeping that trader in a losing position. Price may never go back to that area and then you see your indicators give you conflicting signals. Confusion sets in and the not so smart trader now can't decide on what action to take. This is especially the case if you are trading on the smaller time frames as the decision time is greatly reduced. This is not so much of a problem on 4hr charts and higher though, as you have time to think about your decision and make plans to suit the situation.

18

HYBRID OF METHOD NO. 1 AND METHOD NO. 2

You may even want to consider combining Method No.1 and Method No.2 (a hybrid). By this, I mean you enter your first trade with a carefully considered position size with a normal stop loss in place. If it goes nicely in your favor, then that is great, as you would treat it as a normal trade. But if for whatever reason you are stopped out and price goes against you, then that is fine also. It is a losing trade and that is to be expected every now and then when trading.

But if the MACD Platinum remains on the same side of the zero level and another trade signal presents, you could take this trade with 3x original position size, and again place a carefully considered stop loss.

I will use an example here.

- Let's say you lost -50 pips on your first trade based on 0.1 lot entry.

- This 2nd trade would have been for 0.3 lots, and if it went in your favor of +25 pips, I would close out 0.2 lots, leaving 0.1 lot still in play.

- This +25 pip profit on 0.2 lots would recoup your -50 pip loss based on 0.1 lot.

- Now you are left with your original base lot of 0.1 lot on you 2nd trade.

- If this 2nd trade was stopped out before you had a chance to recover the 1st trade's loss then your 3rd trade if presented, would be for 0.5 lots, where you would look to close out 0.4 lots to recover any previous losses.

▪ If your 2nd trade had recovered the 1st trade's loss, and was therefore reduced to 0.1 lot, then if that was stopped out, your next trade would be for 0.3 lots. The sequence then starts again.

This is simply another way of looking at money management and loss recovery scenarios without getting into too much trouble using multiple trades.

But again, be aware of your money management when selecting position size on your 1st trade (base lot). Also don't be afraid to take a loss, even if it was a little bigger than you expected to take. There will be plenty of new trading signals coming along that will eventually make up for it. With regards to losses, learn from your mistake (if you made one) and then put it out of your mind. Don't get angry and seek revenge. Re-focus and get back in the groove.

Figure 29. Example of a hybrid method using stops

Figure 30. Same chart as Figure 29 but without using stops

19

MANAGING MULTIPLE TRADES

There are many options to manage multiple trades, but this may depend on your broker's requirements under whatever jurisdiction they are based in. For example, a US broker will have to comply with FIFO rules, which basically means that you have to close the trades in the same order you opened them. This can be a little limiting when trying to be a little creative with trade management. The US also limits their traders to a certain leverage, which is currently 50:1 maximum, which is seen by many as a good thing due to the fact that traders are prevented from opening ridiculously huge positions sizes which wouldn't be smart for their account size. This is one of the reasons many unsuccessful traders are in the position they are in, and that is by trading way too big for their account size. The other rule that the US based brokers enforce, is the no hedging rule. So what this means, is that you can't be in a buy trade and a sell trade on the same currency pair at the same time. Not sure how this rule is designed to protect traders, but the powers to be seem to think so. You actually have to be aware of your broker's requirements when doing any type of trading, so that is why it is best to start with your preferred broker's demo (virtual) platform where you can get use to both your trading method and also how the actual platform performs without risking any of your hard earned $$.

I mentioned hedging above. This may be useful when using Method No.2 and you are stuck in a multiple number of trades that are getting a little out of hand, where you may have missed an opportunity to exit, but now are not sure what to do. There may be an ideal scenario where you could start a sequence of trades in the opposite direction to offset any potential losses from the older losing trades. This takes a little bit of thinking and planning as you would then be in multiple positions in both directions, where eventually you are going to have to close out one side or both.

The custom Excel spreadsheet I have provided can help you with this. Here you can input multiple trades in either direction and it will provide you with an overall breakeven price. Or you could copy the spreadsheet and have all of your buy trades on one spreadsheet and all of your sell trades on another one, and treat each basket of trades separately. There are many options here so this spreadsheet can be a very handy tool.

Figure 31. Multiple trades in both directions with positive results

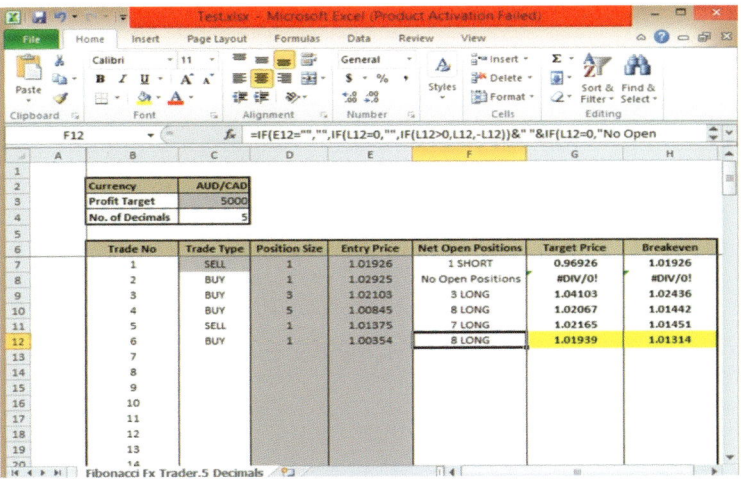

Figure 32. Excel spreadsheet for all of the Figure 31 trades

This particular Excel spreadsheet designed to make life a little easier for me. It is not perfect but it is more than ample for my needs. The first thing I will point out is that it consists of 2 x sheets (found at bottom left) as you can either select 3x decimals or 5x decimals, depending on which pair you are trading. (JPY pairs are all 3x decimals). The box in the top left has an input called 'Profit Target', but you have to add an extra zero to get the correct result.

For example if you were after +200 profit, then you would have to input 2000 in this field.

- The profit is based on your initial lot size.

- In the 'Trade Type' column, the first trade has a drop down menu where you select BUY or SELL, but all the remaining trades, you have to manually type BUY or SELL in there.

- With the 'Position Size' column, there is no need to type in 0.01, 0.03, 0.05 etc as it is fine to type in 1,3,5 etc. As long as you know the ratio comparison.

- You then enter your entry price and the spreadsheet will do the rest, showing you your overall position, profit target and overall breakeven price.

- If you have the exact same number of buy trades and sell trades, where you will be completely hedged, the spreadsheet will show 'No Open Positions' in the 'Net Open positions' column and also jumbled characters in the other two columns to the right.

- When taking the overall breakeven price that is calculated by this spreadsheet into consideration for stop placement, I would be more inclined to add a couple of pips to it if I was long overall, and deduct a couple of pips from it if I was overall short. This will ensure that you will get out at breakeven overall or even slightly better, especially if you have negative swap (interest) involved from holding trades overnight.

A hot tip if trading Method No.2 and you are already in multiple trades; if the MACD Platinum crosses the zero level, I would strongly suggest you immediately move all stops to overall break even or even consider your exit options. Trust me! You do not want to be caught with too many open trades in one direction if at all possible. It is fine if the market is flying off in your preferred direction and you are confident of the big move in your favor. But if the market is meandering it is best to get out at overall break even as a worst case scenario and then re-asses the whole set up. There will be plenty more trades coming along shortly. Patience!

20

CONCLUSION

I have attached a few screenshots of different examples on how to enter and exit, and various other scenarios. But as already stated, this is a framework for your own trading system. Take from this what you wish. There is no EA (as yet) built for this method, nor can I give you a win percentage or how many pips a month you would expect to make etc.

There are so many variables available that it is impossible for me to give specifics. Everyone has their own favorite pairs, timeframes and risk tolerance. If you are new to Forex trading or not sure how this style of trading would work for you, I would suggest using Method No.1, the safer method where each entry is treated as an individual trade. Start off on a demo account and find your own groove and then move up to a live account keeping position size small until you master it. Then you may want to consider Method No.2 or a hybrid of your choice. Once again, I cannot emphasize money management enough and how important it is. This refers to all types of trading, but it is critical when dealing with Method No.2.

So, the method in a nutshell:

Determine a major trend and only trade with that trend, using the MACD Platinum dots for identifying potential trades, and then using the QMP Filter dots for trade entry confirmation.

Place the template on various charts and on various time frames and scroll through them. You will see many potential trading opportunities every day and it will surprise you how simplistic this system is.

Enjoy and all the best with your trading!

If you have any questions or would like to discuss this method, then you are welcome to join my small, newly created Facebook Group at: bit.ly/JAGfx, or contact me on JAGfx33@gmail.com. But before you do, please check out my FAQ section in Google Docs first.

Cheers

Jim

DOWNLOADABLE PACKAGE TO ACCOMPANY THE MT4 HIGH PROBABILITY TRADING METHOD

To download the package, type in the following on your computer:

http://eepurl.com/ca**I**og**1**

(The above is case and space sensitive – note the "I" and the no. "1")

- You will then be required to enter your preferred email for the information to be automatically forwarded to you and you will need to confirm that you are not a "robot".

- If you do not receive the direct link to the folder reasonably quickly (say 10 minutes), please check your spam or trash folder and if it is still not there, don't hesitate to send me an email.

The following files are included in the zip folder:

1. Forex Multiple Trade Calculator.xls
2. i-ParmountWorkTime.mq4
3. MACD Platinum Method.tpl
4. MACD_Platinum.ex4
5. QMP Filter 1.01.ex4
6. QQE ADV.ex4

DOWLOADABLE BOOK IMAGES

Images from the book are downloadable via this link (Google Docs):

http://bit.ly/MT4HP-IMAGES

Keep in mind they are on Australian sized A4, so you may need to adjust the margins if you are printing them.

OTHER BOOKS BY JIM

Forex Trading: The Basics Explained in Simple Terms

Trading Forex with Divergence on MT4

35496570R00037

Printed in Poland
by Amazon Fulfillment
Poland Sp. z o.o., Wrocław